NINE STEPS
TO A
SUCCESSFUL FUNDRAISING CAMPAIGN

LORI L. JACOBWITH

IGNITED
FUNDRAISING

For more information, contact Lori L. Jacobwith, Master Storyteller & Fundraising Culture Change Expert: lori@ignitedfundraising.com

When you use
authentic communication
your supporters give *more*.

— Lori L. Jacobwith

Master Storyteller and Fundraising Culture Change Expert

TABLE OF CONTENTS

INTRODUCTION

Does at least 60% of your philanthropic support come from individual donors?

Do you have an annual donor retention rate of more than 50%? Higher?

Do your individual donors contact YOU to ask, "what else can I do?"

Do more than 25 individuals contribute more than $10,000 annually to your organization?

If you answered "yes" to these questions, you can stop reading. You don't need these nine steps — you're already living by them.

If you answered "no" to any or all of these questions — I wrote this book for you.

After more than 30 years in the social sector as a fundraiser, executive director, trainer, and coach, I've made my share of mistakes. I'd like to share them with you, so you don't have to make them.

Feel free to make your own new and different mistakes.

There are certainly more than nine things you can do to keep donors engaged and actively supporting your mission.

The nine areas this book is focused on are intended to inspire you as you work to increase individual donor giving.

It's my belief that these nine steps are critical to be certain your fundraising campaign or individual program is realizing its full potential.

These steps may shift your focus from fundraising as a mundane task that gets left on the back burner to an inspiring activity. When you and your entire organization are fully engaged in fundraising as a program you will generate considerably more dollars from individuals.

I've kept the story and best practice information in each step brief because I know you're pressed for time.

Read on for my short "soapbox" messages on the key areas of fund development I often find are ignored, forgotten, or simply not being worked thoroughly.

Use these steps as a topic of conversation with your staff, board, volunteers, and even some of your most passionate donors. Add these important topics to meeting agendas and devote time to discussion and implementation.

Some of my favorite source books and tools are listed in the final chapter. I encourage you to check them out to learn more.

Before you dive in let's visit the one common denominator that affects the success of each step: communication.

COMMUNICATION

One main thing creates successful individual donor fundraising: Clear, even bold, COMMUNICATION.

Communication that is powerful and clear is absolutely critical for success. I break communication into four key areas.

1. Sharing Your Story

The way you introduce your organization to others.

What story do you tell people about who you serve and why you exist? Do you tell them what it will take (with people & financial support) to keep doing your important work?

Choosing clear, bold, and emotionally-connecting words will help your organization to stand apart and cause people to take action.

2. Asking

Inviting support without feeling like you are always begging for money.

It sounds simple: just ask people to give their time, talent, stuff, or money to support your organization. The reality: asking for money is both an art and a science. It should only be done by those who do it well, which means not everyone should ask others for a contribution. Providing an invitation for someone to support you is just that, an invitation.

What works best is when the person being asked feels as if their gift will make a big impact.

A good "asker" gets a "yes" often. An excellent asker communicates in such an inspirational way they rarely have to ask. Which are you?

3. Maximizing Relationships

Staying relevant to the people who already support you.

External: Regularly communicate with volunteers and donors to inspire them to stick around. Unfortunately, donor retention in the U.S. has averaged less than 50% for the past 10 or so years.

To entice and inspire donors to stick around will take regular updates about people in your programs. Those updates must clearly show what more there is to do. Pay attention to your regular supporters and communicate so your mission stays relevant for them.

Do you know: Which page on your website is the most visited? Does your newsletter or enews update inspire and teach something new? Do your direct mail and event invitations convey exactly how others can impact one person?

Internal: The way you communicate with your board and staff is where clear and inspiring communication must begin.

Are you clear about expectations in terms of supporting your fundraising efforts?

Do you list specific ways to impact the bottom line; without having to ask for money?

No matter your audience, it's your job to cause them to feel great about their support.

Words matter.

Be intentional about choosing inspiring language rather than utilitarian language. Your goal is simple: Deepen engagement and maximize the relationships you already have.

4. Managing Your Data

What story does your data tell?

The information you maintain about your supporters is key to building institutional memory. It's truly the foundation for sustaining meaningful relationships with your supporters.

Allow your well-maintained donor database to help you know where to focus your time by providing you with:

- Monthly and event-specific retention and acquisition rates.

- Names, contact information, contact history, and giving history of your longest and largest supporters.

Your donor database is as important as the money you have in the bank. Keeping donor records updated is crucial for taking a good development effort and turning it into an exceptional one.

THE common denominator for all four steps is: COMMUNICATION.

Too often nonprofit organizations assume everyone knows what they need in terms of money, time, or staff and board involvement. Usually those assumptions are incorrect.

Open, honest dialogue about each of the following nine steps WILL generate more individual contributions.

Clear communication will also provide increased visibility, clarity of vision, and keep your community inspired.

These steps were designed for groups that:

- Are already a 501(c)(3) organization and able to accept tax-deductible contributions.
- Have already identified programming and are clear how they make a difference to clients, consumers, or members.
- Are interested in learning how, and are willing, to make changes to become more effective in their individual donor communication.

These steps are simple, and you may think you already understand and are using them. I guarantee there are subtleties within each one that will strengthen your individual fundraising program to make it even more successful.

The most successful fundraising professionals focus on the basics first. Then expand into more detailed systems to build their fund development programs. These steps can be used either as your focus on basics OR to move your organization to the next level of fundraising success.

Study and share these case study stories and steps with your board and your staff, and any other key volunteers at your organization.

And please, go ahead, be brave, try things, make mistakes. Just make sure they're new mistakes, not those highlighted by the stories in this book.

STEP# 1

Leadership

Successful individual donor campaigns are led by key volunteer and/or staff leadership.

I am a firm believer in the power of one person.

An effort by one devoted human can make a world of difference in many situations. However, a strong, effective individual donor campaign is not a one-person show.

To put it simply, the long-term work that must be done to cultivate and maintain individual donors requires a considerable amount of time. Yes, one person can devote themselves solely to that task—but if the staff, volunteers, and board members don't support them with additional efforts, your fundraising will not succeed.

If you have the resources for development staff, the CEO/Executive Director and the board chair must be the biggest advocates for that staff.

If you don't have a development staff, the CEO and board chair must take the lead to making sure there is a focus on individual fundraising. I believe it is the responsibility of every person within the organization, whether staff, board, or volunteer, to roll up their sleeves and get involved with fund development.

In most of the nonprofit organizations I come into contact with, nearly everyone shies away from the responsibility of taking care of donors as thoroughly and carefully as they take care of their clients.

Because, as is often the case, when a volunteer or staff is brought on board no one sets expectations for them to participate in development work.

Any time someone is brought into the organization — as a board member, staff, or volunteer — there must be clear and explicit conversations about what's expected of them.

Those expectations might include:

- Soliciting for contributions
- Making a financial contribution themselves
- Giving additional volunteer time
- Making an in-kind contribution
- Serving on the team that makes personal donor thank you calls or sends handwritten notes

Whatever the participation is, that's for your organization to decide. But whatever you decide — make sure everyone knows what is expected.

As you read each story example, don't think I've gone all "Carly Simon" on you; "you probably think this song" — er, story — is about you. It's not.

Or maybe it is.

These stories are based on actual client situations but no real names (human or organization) are used.

STORY **#1** *Leadership*

The board supports the programs — in theory.

Anita is a new board member with Children's Health Foundation. She enthu-siastically joined the board because she feels every child should have access to healthcare.

At her first board meeting Anita found the small endowment of $3.5 million was simply not enough to support the work of the foundation.

The members of the 13-person board all love the organization and are hon-ored to do important work on behalf of children's healthcare. But they were not expected to help raise money as part of serving on this board.

Anita is a young professional in her early 30s and is in favor of raising addi-tional funds. She's not at all daunted by the idea of inviting support from the community for such a worthy reason. Sounds like this might be a great idea, right?

And it is. However, no one has ever had a frank discussion with long-time board members to outline what the expectations are in terms of being involved in fundraising.

The very mention of the word "fundraising" causes sweaty palms and a tight stomach for some. In fact, some of the board members have never made their own financial contribution to Children's Health Foundation. As far as they are concerned, the organization has an endowment generating interest, so there is no need for them to give.

I was brought on to "help."

Within a few months, we determined there needed to be some thoughtful conversations with the board before launching an individual fundraising campaign. Because this was a small office (just 2.5 staff) they were likely going to need to hire a staff person to spearhead their fundraising effort.

As it happens, change takes time. During our meetings and discussions, we uncovered that most of the board members had a deep distaste for talking

about and asking for money.

So much time had passed since Anita and the staff invited me in they, themselves, were no longer as excited about the work ahead. Unfortunately, the endowment declined to the point that they're now in desperate need of individual donors.

While the board is proud of the grants they make, pride alone will not generate financial contributions.

Children's Health Foundation decided to pare back the grants for the time being. They agreed to create an annual board agreement and do some training with the board before they launch their $125,000 annual campaign.

They are moving slowly, but they are moving forward. They are now intentional about expectations. Now this team is working through their fears through ongoing communication.

The good news: the discussion about fundraising has shifted.

New board members are being brought on knowing a personal contribution is part of their board service. Staying in touch with donors is being done on a much more personal level.

Board meetings are spent reviewing retention and acquisition rates of key supporters. And a few individual donor asks have been successful.

All of these changes are setting the stage for a long-term, successful individual donor fundraising effort.

Staff

Successful individual donor campaigns are supported and managed by at least one staff.

For a smaller organization, the sole fundraising staff is often the executive director.

Larger organizations have at least one staff person supporting their fundraising efforts. A team often includes a development director, major gifts officer(s), a grant writer, a database manager, event planning support, and more.

Especially in the early stages of developing an individual fundraising program, it's critical to enlist and encourage others to help with fundraising tasks.

The pool of "workers" can be board members, long-time donors, community volunteers, former staff or board members, and fund development committee members.

There are unlimited tasks to share with others: participating on a solicitation, appeal letter writing, thank you and invitation phone calls, researching donor prospects, planning the annual fundraising event... the list goes on. And on.

When the team is small and concentrated on growth, there is a focus on finding more and more donors. Unfortunately, that often means current donors are neglected.

With an average annual donor retention rate in the U.S. of 48%, it's not a good idea to neglect *any* donors (or volunteers for that matter).

Many smart people I've worked with have made the mistake of putting all their resources into programming.

With a large endowment or large grant from a foundation or corporation can come a level of complacency for fundraising.

We've got plenty right now. Let's worry about securing more money next year or in the final year of multi-year funding support.

I've cringed when I see a new or fast-growing nonprofit focus solely on allocating funds only to their programming and no money or time to fund development. The problem with that is clear:

No funds coming in = no new programs going out.

If your organization is serious about continuing to provide quality services supporting the **program** of fund development is necessary.

Programs and services have managers and staff to implement your amazing work, so must your individual donor program have a person to keep your mission and donors' impact relevant and visible.

It's tempting during economic downtimes to reduce or cut funding staff altogether. But that very short-term solution will create long-term problems.

STORY **#2** *Staff*

I'll do it. All of it.

I'm honored to work alongside visionary, inspiring men and women who are often founders of their organization.

Their vision and dedication amazes and inspires me.

Beth is a founder who has been incredibly successful securing funding from the federal government for medical research.

Unfortunately, she's been ineffective raising any operating funds. Zero is the operating budget for an organization with $10 million research dollars.

Beth's desire to "do it all herself" has stalled the growth of this important organization.

Beth doesn't yet receive a salary. She's the public face of the organization, often speaking to large groups in the medical community. Slowly a buzz has begun to simmer about outcomes from research the ABC organization has funded.

What's missing?

- *Regular communication with their handful of supporters.*
- *Messaging that inspires more involvement and unrestricted contributions.*
- *1:1 donor solicitation meetings.*
- *Building a strong board.*
- *Engaging community members in a committee structure.*
- *A regular paycheck for Beth's more than full-time work.*

The first thing we agreed on is that Beth SHOULD be receiving a salary. Doing all that she does and struggling to make ends meet is currently a hidden cost of running this organization.

Next, we agreed to refresh and reframe messages Beth shares. The best way to stand out in the barrage of communication we all wade through every day is to share an inspiring vision for the future.

Beth wasn't talking about the size of the budget. Nor did she talk about what it takes to manage any of the research grants they've been awarded.

Digging deeper, I found, Beth wasn't actually sure how much time or financial resources managing the grants took. Once we determined those costs, Beth began, slowly, to share a much more inspiring vision.

After multiple conversations about what it would take to grow exponentially, Beth agreed to ask for specific help.

She began inviting passionate supporters to be an ambassador for the ABC organization. When her invitations become more specific, Beth found it easier than she ever imagined to find people willing to volunteer. She invited them to share the newly crafted visionary messages at house parties, via social media and email.

Beth and the board are more transparent about what it will take to "do more." A clear vision for growth is being shared everywhere.

Since making these changes the ABC organization has increased their unrestricted operating budget to nearly $100,000.

So far, they have more than 300 **new** donors.

Beth is being paid a small salary with a timeline to pay her a market rate salary within two years.

At least one volunteer ambassador per state has been recruited and trained in the U.S.

A simple communication plan has increased the frequency and clarity of communication. This allows people to regularly see a place for themselves to make a meaningful impact with their time **and** money.

Most importantly, today, Beth doesn't have to do it "all."

Board Members

Successful individual donor campaigns have all board members participating in fundraising in some capacity (and I don't mean the "Hey, you're doing a great job" cheerleading role).

Being a board member is not a simple invitation to bestow on people who show up at meetings. Full board participation is critical to the growth, effectiveness, and financial success of your organization.

I can feel cringes and eye rolls as I write this.

I bet I can read your mind, too: "But Lori, you don't know *my* organization — my board can't/won't agree to give more time or money."

Or, "Our board wasn't recruited to ask for money. I can't ask them to ask others."

Or, "Our board is appointed and can't do fundraising."

The reality is, without FULL board participation and a clear understanding of the fundraising program, your vision of doing more is far more difficult.

What's the best way to engage board members to support your fundraising work?

Recruit with an expectation and accountability discussion. When someone is invited to *consider* joining the board use clear communication about expectations. How? Use a board agreement that is filled out annually. (A link to a free ebook with a sample board agreement is provided in the resources chapter.)

Before recruiting any new board members, ask yourself if you are providing the following:

- A job description with the board role clearly defined.

- Specific expectations for board members to help raise awareness, and for some, raise money.

- Ongoing training to do any aspect of their board role.

Most importantly do you have at least one advocate on your board who supports efforts to create a successful and engaged board?

Here's what I mean: In the interview process it's critical that both fundraising (the raising of assets) and fund development (raising of visibility and deepening engagement) activities be thoroughly discussed and outlined. New board members must know beyond any doubt that they will be included in the "doing" as well as the giving.

A frequent mistake I encounter is that the development staff is not specific enough — because they haven't discussed it or created a plan around it — about what they want from board members. The board is left to figure out on their own how to "engage" themselves.

It's as though you want me to know how to scuba dive because I love being in the water, but no one ever takes the time to teach me how to do it.

This doesn't mean board members have to spend all their free time directly asking for financial contributions.

In fact, if they aren't good at it, a board member should not ask others for money.

Here are some best practices to follow that will increase your fundraising revenue while engaging board members (and volunteers) in supporting the program of fundraising:

1. **Make a financial contribution** of any size. 100% board giving is non-negotiable.

2. **Regularly show up** to board and committee meetings. Agree on attendance requirements with the board and track it.

3. **Invite others to events**, including the "get to know us" free events. Track this by board member and share at board meetings.

4. **Truly act as an ambassador** by knowing the names and faces of the top 25 to 50 donors and volunteers. Then seek them out at events to thank and talk with them.

5. **Make a thank you phone call** to recent donors. Research from Penelope Burk indicates when a board member or volunteer phones to thank a first-time donor their second gift increases by nearly 39%. That's fundraising!

6. **Meet with a current or former donor** to thank them for their recent gift. It's not practical to take every donor out; set a minimum donation gift level for this activity.

7. **Make an introduction** to the community affairs person at their workplace.

8. **Secure a matching gift** from their workplace. Often this is as simple as a reminder to fill out a form.

9. **Share a story** about one person's life that's different because of your organization.

10. **Deliver a heartfelt — but short — speech** at their place of worship or civic group meeting to stir up interest in your organization.

11. **Know and regularly share with others your "money story."** This means talking about inspirational and visionary fundraising goals using language like, "Here's what it will take to say yes more often."

12. **Host a house party** to introduce their passion for your organization to their community.

13. **Write a short article** about why your mission is their passion for social media or your enews.

14. **Hold themselves and each other accountable** for what they said they would do.

———

A quick note about action 5: Making thank you phone calls to donors is not just a nice gesture. It has been shown to increase giving **and** engage the board at a much deeper level.

In my coaching I make the task of thank you calls an important requirement for every board or development committee meeting.

Here's how:

- In less than 10 minutes each person is provided with one or two donors to call to thank. *Make sure the numbers work ahead of time.*

- Always have a staff member or someone who is comfortable making a call do the first one to show the board how simple it is.

- Remind them to take notes for your data management system (more on that later).

- Some will likely be nervous about it at first. That's okay.

- Remind them their call will likely go to voice mail.

- Be clear that their thank you message to a donor has the power to increase the next contribution AND keep that donor feeling special enough to give again for up to two more years.

I've watched people with sweaty palms dial their first call; have a lovely short conversation with a passionate donor; and then turn around and ask for more names because they enjoyed it so much.

———

This is a short list of the many ways board members can actively participate in fundraising activities — *without* having to ask others for money.

No matter which activity is chosen, make certain expectations are clear well ahead of time.

Discussion about "which of our own activities should we track?" is an excellent annual retreat topic.

The role of staff (when there is staff) is to assist by regularly providing accurate data so board members can hold themselves accountable for what they said they would do.

STORY **#3** *Board Members*

My board won't help with fundraising.

I hear this comment often.

Honestly, over the years, I've become a skeptic about the reality of this statement.

More often than not, when I enter the picture and begin working with board members I encounter passionate, committed professionals. They don't want to do anything wrong. When asked to do something outside their comfort zone some wait for clear direction.

I believe every board member shows up wanting to be successful and make a difference. After a meeting or two the current board culture takes over.

When there are no consequences for lack of attendance at meetings or events; no follow-up about the signed board agreement; and no training in areas that are key for raising awareness, e.g. sharing a mission moment story; board members tune out, get bored and disengage.

A few years ago, Leslie invited me to facilitate an annual board retreat for a veterans' advocacy organization. The intended outcome was re-engaging and deeply connecting the board after a large capital campaign.

Leslie assured me there would be lots of push back and not to have very high expectations of the board.

I did my "prep" work with the board chair, Wayne, and found him to be a smart, professional business owner and veteran. He and Leslie shared their concerns about donor and especially board fatigue after the completion of a $24-million capital campaign.

When I asked Wayne why he thought the board had disengaged after such a successful campaign he candidly said, "Lori, we don't know what to do next. Most of us are thankful we can stop asking for big gifts. Frankly, we need a break from fundraising."

I paused and said, "Wayne, I understand the fatigue. You worked hard over the past three years.

What if I told you that when the board takes a break from talking with donors — not asking — connecting with them — you'll see a huge drop off in active donors?

But I have some ideas about how to keep donors connected without having to ask for money."

Now I had his attention. "Go on," he said.

"Let's make the retreat a celebration of all the ways it was a success: number of donors, size of gifts, increases in giving and so on," I said. "But how about I also facilitate a conversation about what will keep them giving?"

Wayne's eyes lit up.

He nodded and said, "We haven't really celebrated our own success as a board. And we certainly have never talked about what makes the same people want to give to the annual fund too."

As a business owner Wayne was energized when we talked about the importance of knowing and managing the retention and acquisition rate of donors. Leslie readily agreed to have her staff pull together data and charts that would tell a story about where to focus for the coming six to 12 months.

I invited Wayne to be an active partner in making sure the retreat was a success. He agreed to move things along during the discussions and to help to keep people accountable for attending the session and being on time.

What I modeled for Leslie was to be as specific as possible in engaging Wayne in the areas where he excels.

The four-hour session turned out better than Leslie and Wayne imagined. We had robust discussions about ways to keep donors engaged.

Everyone had an opportunity to share a short mission moment about how their advocacy work affects the life of a veteran they had met.

We reviewed the success of the recent capital campaign and five years of annual fund fundraising outcomes using fun, easy-to-understand visuals.

When I asked the question: "How might this board help to keep current donors engaged?" Discussion ended with agreement that the board would focus on these specific areas:

1. *Quarterly donor retention increases of 3-5% per quarter.*

2. *Inspire current donors of $5000+ to give again through a series of touch points:*

    *   *Monthly email updates from the board chair about the impact of their gifts. The emails would highlight a short mission moment video clip.*

    *   *Small VIP mission-focused gathering (bill signings, testimony preparation of veterans, visits to facilities benefiting from legislation).*

    *   *Personal thank you calls to donors on the anniversary of their capital gift that include an inspiring mission moment and an update on the current annual funding gap.*

3. *Monitor progress regularly at board, committee, and staff meetings.*

There was excitement and a sense of possibility at the retreat. I credit some of the success to the board chair, Wayne. He helped keep discussions focused and drew out some of the quiet and newer board members.

When I checked back with them a few months later they had already seen more than 10% retention increase. Fifty-percent of capital campaign donors had already stepped up to make a contribution to the annual fund.

The staff keeps busy providing clean data and fun visuals at committee and board meetings.

But what was even more exciting to learn, was that more board members are attending and inviting donors to events.

I was proud to learn there has been a total turnaround in board support for fundraising activities.

Goals, Timelines, and Urgency

Successful individual donor campaigns have a well-defined goal, with a specific timeline, creating a sense of urgency.

Set goals — and tell people about them.

Every organization, no matter their size, requires financial support.

Some set specific fundraising goals based on their annual budget. Others set their goals based on annual fundraising plans that carefully plot their vision for growth.

General operating fundraising support comes from corporations, foundations, and individual donors. Some organizations receive funding from government contracts and fees for service. No matter where the financial support is from, the reality is all organizations could do more with more money.

Being clear about why and "by when" causes people to give more.

One organization I've worked with generates more than 50,000 new donors each year. Contributions range from $5 to hundreds of thousands. Nearly all their contributions are made online.

Unfortunately, their annual donor retention rate is less than 25%.

I know — you'd like to have the problem of having 50,000 annual donors.

What *you do not want* is to be in a position to have to replace 75% of your donors each year. It's simply too time-consuming and costly.

How do you keep current donors connected so they keep contributing?

In Step 5 we'll talk more about the emotional connection to increase donor retention.

This step is about the importance of creating a sense of urgency by being specific.

It's helpful to break an annual goal down into smaller mini-campaigns to maintain a sense of urgency.

If $30,000 will make a significant difference this month, share that. If you are focusing on increasing your pool of $1000-a-year donors by 100 this year, share that.

Be clear "what it will take" to reach your next milestone for the growth, but always attach a "by when" to create the sense of urgency.

Whenever sharing examples of specific size gifts and how they will help a real person: scholarships, passing a law, creating a match between a rescue animal and a human, researching a drug, or teaching a vet a new skill... be specific.

Most importantly, do not wait until the final quarter of the year to tell donors that you have not met your goal.

Keeping stakeholders updated throughout the year by blending your fundraising updates with stories about the impact their gift will have on one person is the key.

Talking about what you need doesn't compel. Talking about "what it takes" is more inspiring — especially for your most passionate supporters.

STORY **#4** *Goals, Timelines, and Urgency*

We need money NOW.

A terrific organization, Ready Set Go, works to provide employment training for people who've lost their jobs and found themselves in a financial crisis.

Their cash reserve had shrunk while waiting for two large grants to be approved. When the grants eventually were declined, there simply was not enough money for more than a month's payroll.

At a mid-March fundraising meeting with key leadership and staff I asked the question: If cash flow is so dire why are we not inviting people to contribute?

As it turned out, Ready Set Go had never done a spring appeal. Their tiny but mighty staff didn't have skills to make one-on-one donor solicitations.

In the past they had relied solely on one mail and one email message in December to invite supporters to make a financial contribution. While they were able to raise more than $75,000 in December they were relying on grants for 80% of their annual budget.

Our discussion determined an emergency fundraising goal of $40,000 to get them to the end of August when they would receive checks for two grants that were renewed for a second year.

We quickly cooked up a plan:

- *Secure a $20,000 matching gift ASAP from donors with the longest giving history.*

- *Draft and send 4 email solicitations about "what it takes to support one client" (a real person) in their program.*

- *Update the home page and donate page on the website with one of the client stories, matching gift updates, and the deadline of May 31 to raise $40,000.*

- *A two-page direct mail appeal that included one of the stories from the email campaign.*

- *A two-evening volunteer phone-a-thon.*

- *Twice weekly social media updates using similar language, photos, and stories from the email solicitations.*

- *Five days after the deadline of June 1: One follow-up email, multiple social media posts, and a website update to report on how the campaign had done.*

Our communication was spread out over six weeks.

The good news was Ready Set Go had more than 4000 supporters in their database. Unfortunately, they found that many of their longest giving donors did not have email addresses.

First things first: They invited two groups of youth from local high schools in need of service projects. These eager teens helped collect accurate phone numbers, email addresses, and mailing addresses for as many of the 4000 records as possible. Within two weeks they had a great list.

Our Communication Guidelines:

- *Short, compelling, 250-word or less email messages that would include a short story about a real client.*

- *All messages provided specific examples of how a specific dollar amount ($75 to $1000) would make a difference.*

- *All messages conveyed a sense of urgency by mentioning the $20,000 matching gift that would expire on June 1.*

- *Email messages had up to three links to* **Make a Difference** *and connected to the website giving page.*

- *The home page and donate page on their website were updated to reflect daily updates on donor count and total dollars given to the campaign.*

Results

The first email generated a few hundred dollars from four people.

The second email generated nearly $6000 from more than 40 people.

The third email brought the total giving to over $11,000. More than half was from new donors.

Next the direct mail message dropped, and money began to arrive daily. Small amounts of $5 and $10 all the way to $2500 were sent via mail.

The week of the mailing we set aside two evenings to conduct a volunteer phone-a-thon. We made this a fun event with pizza, a tally board, and we rang a bell each time a caller got a yes.

After the evening of phone calls total gifts reached nearly $80,000 — double the original goal! Cash flow was no longer an issue.

The last report I heard from Ready Set Go was they received more than $100,000 in contributions — nearly 75% of which was "new" money.

The plan is to never go back to only asking for financial support once a year. The spring appeal using multiple forms of communication became the model to use in the fall.

Staff committed to regularly updating donors and volunteers about the impact of previous gifts. They've been providing updates about gift sizes that were the most common during that fundraising effort for years.

They now share updates about waiting lists and quarterly fundraising milestones.

What they actually committed to without realizing it is to be specific and create a sense of urgency — all year long — allowing their donors to be inspired and know exactly what is needed.

STEP # 5

Telling Your Story

Successful individual donor campaigns create an emotional connection — making it personal for people to participate.

Make me care.

It's time to talk about my passion: **sharing emotionally engaging stories**.

By sharing a real-life example of the impact and value of your work you paint a picture of my impact as a donor.

Our brains are wired to think in story. We tell ourselves stories to make a decision. We share stories with others to feel connected.

Donors may not always remember the facts about how many people are homeless in your city. They ARE likely to remember the feeling they had about the story of a mother who helps her son do his homework in the car using the dome light.

The most powerful way to bring any mission alive is to tell a story about someone whose life is different because of your work.

Your goal is to cause the person listening or reading to feel something, which often translates to feelings of empathy.

Stories that create sympathy are distance-causing.

Stories that create empathy are emotionally connecting.

Feeling emotionally connected is the first step to taking action.

By sharing powerful stories, you cause people to care enough that they realize they can't sit by on the sidelines watching and doing nothing.

Sharing pages of statistics about the increase in homelessness due to the economy can become mind-numbing.

Talking about Marcus, a 52-year-old man who was "downsized" from his sales job and now works as a cashier at a gas station makes homelessness real.

He can't afford rent so sometimes he sleeps on a friend's couch. When they say no he stays at a homeless shelter. He's even had to resort to sleeping on park benches.

To stay clean, he showers at friend's houses or uses the sink at work. When asked how this all feels he's said, "I'm ashamed and embarrassed. I don't even want to let people see me, so I don't look them in the eye most days."

Then share what happened when your staff and volunteers helped Marcus find dignity by finding temporary housing. Share how he feels about being "seen" and supported for the first time in years.

It is clear which approach will be more successful. Statistics without a story makes people's eyes glaze over.

A haunting story of Marcus, a man trying to make it in a tough world who could be the person they saw at the gas station today, is an example of a mission moment.

I define a mission moment as a real-life example of your work in action.

5 Essential Storytelling Secrets

1. **Make your story about one person.**
   Stories told in a way that connects listeners or readers to a single person allows them to see themselves in the story AND your mission.

2. **When sharing a story out loud, shorter is better.**
   Cause the listener or reader to want to know even more about your organization. Sharing a short, powerful example of your work should cause others to ask you a question about the person you're talking about.

3. **Share exact results AND transformations for the person in your story.**
   Exact results are things you can measure about one person's experience with you. They have a home, a degree, a new job, they are safe, they attended a concert, acted in play, or helped clean up the river.

   Transformations are how that person now feels: Capable, strong, smart, hopeful for the very first time.

4. **Clearly define the conflict.**
   Conflict is the oxygen in your story. There is always a villain. It may be an illness, contaminated water, loss of a job, or not being able to afford to learn to play an instrument.

5. **Use emotionally engaging words.**
   When we pause and choose inspiring and inviting language that engages our supporters we open up opportunities for deeper connections and bigger actions.

Where to share stories? Everywhere and anywhere.

I'm amazed at how many organizations don't share a story on the home page or the contribution page of their website. A photo and short example of a how life is different for someone because of your work causes a deeper connection. It's that deeper connection that keeps people giving.

Start staff and board meetings with a mission moment story. Share them in newsletters, at special events, at donor stewardship meetings, at volunteer recruitment gatherings, the list goes on.

People are looking to "feel" something and you've got the magical opportunity to cause them to feel something whenever you are in contact with them.

It's important to remember your board, volunteers, and donors do not regularly come into contact with real-life examples of the children, men and women you serve.

The very best way to share a story is for the person who it's about to tell it. However, live testimonials don't always fit into the agenda or timeline. So, start strengthening your storytelling muscle to tell and write short, compelling examples of your work.

An important note: Use the two-minute rule. Minds start to wander quickly so keep your story telling and real-life examples short and packed with an emotional punch.

No matter how large your goal is — whether it's to stop hunger in Africa, lobby for more education funding, educate poverty-stricken children all over the U.S., or preserve crumbling artworks in a small-town museum — drill down to the story of one: one person, one animal, one saved masterpiece — one specific instance.

With just one, you've got far more opportunity to build that emotional connection because your supporters can then visualize the example you are sharing.

STORY #5 *Telling Your Story*

Real stories.

The truth is I often find myself cringing when I read most so-called stories.

Rarely is time taken to teach how to tell an engaging story. Staff and board members are expected to just know how to do it.

Unfortunately, what many call a story is often no more than reciting a list of facts. Without painting a picture or using descriptive words, the story becomes little more than "noise" or message clutter.

Fortunately, Joshua, the CEO of a large human service organization, agrees with me about training others to deliver powerful stories.

Joshua wanted to inspire his board members to be more active ambassadors. He invited me to provide storytelling training to his 20 board members.

I explained to Joshua that I could certainly teach the mechanics of storytelling, but it would be more rewarding for each board member to first meet a client. That way they would have experienced first-hand a personal connection.

Every board member worked with the development staff to schedule a meeting with a client in their personal area of interest. Because the organization had so many different programs it was easy to ensure each board member met a different person.

Once the scheduled training session was finished, it was clear these were exceptionally passionate and articulate board members.

At a board meeting a few months later Joshua invited one board member to attend a meeting with a program officer from the community foundation. Joshua was clear he only wanted one board member to join him. He was surprised that three wanted to attend the meeting.

Each board member made it clear they had a terrific story that should be heard by the program officer. Rather than dash their enthusiasm Joshua agreed to bring all three to the meeting.

The meeting was to introduce the idea of a $250,000 grant — the largest grant they had ever requested from this foundation. The money would be used as a matching gift for an upcoming event.

Joshua specifically asked the board members to keep their stories to two minutes or less to allow him time to cover how the grant would leverage more money at their event.

What unfolded was not exactly what was planned but turned out to be incredibly effective. After preliminary introductions each of the board members took turns talking about "their person." They wanted the program officer to understand how the grant would affect him or her.

The hour-long meeting ended with Joshua barely able to get a word in, and he told me he was worried.

Before ending the meeting, the program officer said, "Joshua, you are fortunate to have such passionate and knowledgeable board members. Never before have I seen board engagement like this, for that reason I will be recommending we fund your request in full."

This is just one example of literally hundreds I could share with you that highlight the power of authentic, emotionally-engaging stories in action.

STEP # 6
Keeping Your Donors Engaged

Successful individual donor campaigns keep donors and interested parties informed and engaged.

In other words: Communicate!

As soon as a donor or volunteer shares their gifts of time or money with you — it's now your responsibility to maintain a meaningful connection.

How do you keep them engaged and wanting to know more?

As staff, think about how often you come into contact with your mission in action.

While you may not talk with any concert attendees (though I believe you *should*), you see enjoyment or relaxation on their face during a performance.

While you may not be a case manager or deliver programming, you have the opportunity to walk into an area of your building and see the face of a client.

Maybe you aren't the person at the legislature advocating for the bill to be passed, but you may help find people to give their testimony at a hearing.

The reality is, the outside community and even some of your key volunteer leadership don't come into regular contact with your mission in action on a regular basis.

Our job is to keep the impact of contributions visible to donors and volunteers in between asking them for support.

There is *always* something to share.

Even the smallest example of change can inspire when shared in an emotionally-connecting way.

The key to success for life and for nonprofit organizations is to maintain regular communication.

Keep information flowing through in-person meetings, direct mail, email, phone, websites, and social media. Staying in touch has never been easier.

The truth to why your donors stop giving is they lose interest. They don't feel their gift matters enough to keep giving it.

I recently spoke with staff at a large, seemingly successful nonprofit. I was shocked to discover that other than a thank you letter or email after a contribution, *there is no other communication with donors until it's time to ask for another gift.* Yikes!

I spoke at a panel about this topic in front of nearly 600 people. I was disappointed to learn **more than two thirds of the organizations represented in the room** — some having 2000, 5000, and even 8000 active donors — **were very concerned about meeting their annual fundraising goals** but they **could not tell me their donor retention rate or the names of their top 20 donors.**

My belief: If you have a donor retention issue, you have a communication issue.

Building your donor list is important, agreed. If your donor retention rate is below 60% or you're worried about meeting year-end goals — **you are not paying enough attention to your current donors.**

Meanwhile, people who invested their money or time in you are leaving. It's no surprise donor retention in the U.S. has been less than 50% for the past 15 years.

Five tips for keeping your donors happy, connected to your mission, and giving more.

1. **Share how contributions make an impact for one person.**
   How many of your current donors & volunteers understand clearly

what it is you raise money for? Do you share the cost of your programs for one week for one child or one adult?

A friend who is a major donor recently told me, "If the organizations I support were not just saying they need money but telling me why and what impact that money will have, I'd give even more."

2. **Throughout the year: Personally contact as many donors as you can who give multiple times a year or for multiple years.**
   You can use board members, community volunteers, and even donors to help you.

   Contacts can be thank you calls, invitation calls, or simply a "getting to know more about you" call or meeting.

   NOTE: The person doesn't have to say "yes" to the meeting or answer the call for it to be meaningful. Leaving a warm thank you message is more powerful than you realize.

3. **Meaningful acknowledgement can have a huge impact on your pipeline.**
   This means timely, meaningful thank you letters AND more. Get creative with how you stay connected to your supporters: Shout outs on social media, sending an ecard for their birthday or on the anniversary of their first gift.

4. **Invitations to events should say more than "Join us or Attend!"**
   Share a compelling reason for guests to attend and remind them of the need in your community.

———

Excellent "mission-focused" example of copy on a fundraising event invitation: *One in four homeless men in our community is a veteran. We think ONE is too many.*

———

At any event, share an update on the current gap in where your funding is vs. where your funding must be to say yes more often to the communities you serve.

Couple this with a compelling story about how amazing your programs are. If you only show all the "good work" and positive outcomes donors don't see a reason to do more.

5. **Regular communication ALL YEAR LONG that is compelling and shows your impact has huge value in both retaining and generating new donors.**
   Even a small increase in donor retention will generate greater dollars raised over time. Adrian Sargeant, Ph.D., from Indiana University's Center on Philanthropy says:

   "A 10% increase in donor retention can increase the lifetime value of the donor database up to 200%. When people stay around they do things like upgrade their gifts, [give more often], contribute to galas and even volunteer."

Remember: Regular communication does not have to be lengthy.

Short, interesting emails, with subject lines that beg to be opened are a good start.

Make certain those short messages teach something new, inspire, and invite action.

Monthly giving is one of the very best ways to increasing donor retention. Monthly gifts give you an important reason to stay in touch and remind donors of the impact of their regular support.

If you don't believe me, maybe this will inspire you: Annual donor retention of monthly donors averages 90% in the U.S. Wow!

STORY #6 *Keeping Your Donors Engaged*

Keeping donors informed and engaged.

Success, it's been said, is in the details.

I attended a fundraising committee meeting as a volunteer for a nonprofit whose budget had shrunk to less than half over a two-year period.

Helen, the executive director, asked for my help. I agreed to attend the meeting, provide candid feedback, and share resources. I told her I would consider taking on tasks to help in any way I could. In fact, before I left, I made a $100 contribution online.

But, wait, let's back up... here's the ugly truth:

- *There's been staff turnover at the Executive Director level, twice in the past three years.*
- *The board is not at 100% board giving.*
- *There is no fundraising staff. Any and all fundraising is done by the Executive Director, when she has time.*

Back to our meeting.

Just two out of five committee members showed up: one board member and me. Three board members were no shows.

Putting on my "caring truth-teller" hat at our one-hour meeting we ended with these outcomes:

1. *Agreement on a goal to raise $70k within two months.*
2. *A plan to send an appeal letter within two weeks — that I would draft within two days.*
3. *Agreement to review donor lists and make phone calls to invite a matching gift.*
4. *Feeling of a clear focus and an action plan.*

And then... crickets.

I sent my recommended draft of an appeal letter by the agreed deadline — then heard nothing.

Even though each of us in attendance agreed to take on specific actions more than three weeks went by without any follow-up. As a volunteer and a donor for more than 10 years, I was annoyed and sad.

This young, eager, over-worked staff person did not use the talented willing committee to ease her overwhelm.

There was not even a whisper of communication to donors during weeks prior to the appeal letter being mailed. No inspiring mission moment stories were shared. No updates about the current funding situation. No exciting vision for the future.

When the appeal was finally sent out, nearly a month later, the results were dismal. I was told the board got their hands on the letter and watered down the message, removed the language about their funding gap, and there was no inspiring matching gift.

When I reached out to Helen about the parts of the plan that weren't acted on she said, "There simply isn't time to call donors or send newsletter updates right now. We have to get our programs up and running for the fall."

No surprise the budget continued to shrink. Engagement from the board, donors, and volunteers continued to wane. Eventually the organization shut down.

While this is an extreme outcome for not staying in touch with — this is a true story.

Money Conversation

Successful individual donor campaigns keep your money story visible to encourage widespread participation.

Keep all eyes on the goal.

Quickly, do you know exactly where your organization is, today, in meeting your annual fundraising goals?

Does everyone on the staff and the board?

Do you talk about your "growth" budget with your board and your donors?

Are you regularly sharing your vision for making a bigger impact and what that will take financially?

Are you basing your annual budget on a small increase over what you raised last year?

Recommendation

Base your fundraising goals on what it actually takes to do your work vs. what you think people will give.

Having a balanced budget throughout the year is key, I agree. Equally important is helping your community understand there is more to do. And the "more to do" takes more resources.

After more than 30 years of raising or helping organizations raise more than $300 million I know the formula for exceeding annual fundraising goals:

1. Educating donors about the impact of previous gifts.
2. Highlighting the life of one person.
3. Regularly sharing your money story.

———

Your "money story" is the gap between where you are today in reaching your annual fundraising goals AND your visionary — forward thinking — fundraising goal vs. the amount you've raised so far this year.

———

Annual funding gap messages and visionary fundraising goals kept private and hidden leave money on the table.

If, to be effective, you MUST become a $1 million or $10 million or $100 million organization — share that vision regularly.

Whenever possible, make certain the visionary goal and timeline are exciting by sharing it in unique, engaging, even fun ways.

If you know it will take $1 million to do your work effectively then say that — even if your actual budget is $450k this year.

How? Something like this: *We are on a mission to be a $1 million organization, so we can say yes to more people like [name of someone real]. Today we have a gap of nearly $520k before we reach that milestone.*

The key is to remind supporters where you're at *today*, so they know when you ask for another gift an increased contribution WILL make a difference.

Two Parts to Finding Your Money Story for Your Nonprofit

1. Know the gap between where you are today in reaching your annual fundraising goals vs. what you've received from contributions, ticket sales, fees, government, United Way funding, etc.

Only share what's in the door — not what is expected. By sharing what you "expect" to raise, you remove any sense of urgency for giving.

2. Know the gap between where you are in reaching your visionary fundraising goal(s) and what your annual budget is today.

Massive fundraising results requires telling the truth.

Calculate your visionary fundraising goal by answering these questions:

*   How many people do we say no to weekly, monthly, annually?

*   Where are we cutting to the bone to keep our spending down?

*   What should we be doing more of and why?

*   What will all of this cost?

STORY #7 *Money Conversation*

Sharing your money story.

Years ago, before facilitating a board retreat for a hospital foundation, I took the tour of the hospital.

The tour was for new staff, so it was thorough and included a number of stops throughout the hospital.

At each stop, the department head shared examples of the importance of their work, a few startling statistics, and then we had a few minutes to ask questions.

My questions for each department head were:

- *What is the most important, and possibly invisible to others, work your department does?*

- *What needs to be replaced in your department?*

- *What do you need to do your work safer, better, or more efficiently?*

In less than half a day I knew why the hospital was such a quality place. I also had a good idea of the amount of their visionary fundraising goal.

At the board retreat I shared stories about some of the best kept secrets of each department. Included in each example was a dollar amount about what it would take to provide more exceptional care for patients.

The trustees were curious how I appeared to "know more than they did."

Executive and Development Directors who shy away from sharing their money story often feel talking about a large "funding gap" will cause people to think the organization is not run well.

I believe the exact opposite.

I've watched, over and over again, as organizations that are transparent about costs, goals, and the human impact of a gift create committed donors willing to give more.

Be Specific

Successful individual donor campaigns invite participants to do very specific things with a deadline for doing them.

You can't be too specific when it comes to communicating about your organization's needs and goals.

Far too many fundraising or board meetings happen without coming to an agreement on a plan.

Far too many fundraising appeals ask for help without explaining what the help will accomplish.

It's like when my nine-year-old niece called and said, "Auntie, will you please buy a chocolate bar?" I bought one chocolate bar, because she's my niece.

If she had told me the money raised will help fifteen students attend her drama camp, I might have bought the whole box.

More of anything only shows up when people are crystal clear about what is needed to make a difference.

This step is as much about raising money as it is inspiring your board and donors to do more.

If people are not doing what you need or want them to do, start doing better follow up.

Then ask YOURSELF:

- What am I doing to inspire others to support me and/or this organization?

- How specific and clear am I being about what actions will make a significant difference?

- And most importantly, how quickly am I following up with calls, information, or notes to keep the momentum going?

Whether it's with a donor ask, a board member helping with an event, or your staff getting their work done, **spurring others into taking action starts with YOU**.

A powerful tool to use to get others to do what you want is the Sample Meeting Note Format found on the free resources page of my website (see link in the resources section).

You might say, I don't have time to send out such detailed meeting notes.

You don't have time NOT TO.

STORY **#8** *Be Specific*

Being specific makes a difference.

Dear Lori,

As a longtime donor you know we work hard to ensure our resources go directly to support victims of domestic abuse and we keep our overhead costs low.

Recent thunderstorms produced rain inside some of our rooms where anxious mothers and children meet for group therapy. Since these rooms help them rebuild their lives, we concluded this was an "overhead" expense we couldn't ignore.

We are inviting you to help us with this unexpected "overhead" expense.

Our new roof costs $25,000. That's 1,000 shingles at $25 each. If 1000 supporters each add a shingle, we're snug and dry for the winter! Or, if 250 of you add four shingles each. Or... you get the idea.

But, wait! There's more!

On Tuesday, November 17, beginning at 8 am, all contributions to Raise the Roof will count double thanks to the generosity of our board matching gift pool. So, two shingles can become four. Ten shingles become 20.

Your investment will go farther than on any other day!

In this real example, donors were invited to help in a big or small way. We were invited to something specific, within a specific timeline, for a specific reason.

Since anonymity of clients was important, in the email we were shown a blurred silhouette of a child holding hands with his therapist in a therapy room. The caption on the photo read, "While you may never meet seven-year-old Sinclair, your roof shingles will help him heal from seeing his mother being beaten."

Any time a vivid picture is painted for the impact of a contribution, a deeper connection is created.

There was not a DONATE button in the email appeal. The button actually said, **I'll Help Raise the Roof.**

Results of the campaign, I later learned, **exceeded the goal by more than triple — within just five days.** *Making this the most successful fundraising campaign the organization had ever had to that point.*

When I asked Sandy, the development director, what she learned from this fast and furious effort, her answer was, "Be specific!"

Donor Data Management

Successful individual donor campaigns use a donor data management system to track donor contacts and gifts.

Your data is as important as money in the bank.

A well-maintained data tracking system can mean the difference between meeting your financial goals or not.

Eventually, spreadsheets become cumbersome, limited in functionality, and you have multiple versions of the same data.

Saying your organization *can't afford* a way to keep track of your institutional memory is not an effective business practice.

A good fundraising database should help you track what you're doing and what you've received. It should track your contributions, pledges, solicitations, donors, volunteers, event attendees, and more.

A well-maintained system will help you monitor and forecast performance.

Your fundraising database should also help you focus your work, manage your time, and ask the right person for the right gift at the right time.

A system where everyone is trained to enter information is invaluable in mining for deeper commitments from your supporters.

Due to the efficiency of what you know about your data, a well-maintained database is like adding a part-time person to your team.

Here are questions your donor data will help you answer:

- Who has given for multiple years?

- Who has given in different years at $100+? $500+? $1000+?

- How many times have you been in touch with those donors by mail? Email? Phone?

- When was the most recent contact and by whom?

- Who at your organization knows those specific donors or volunteers?

- Who gave to you last year but unfortunately not yet this year? (LYBUNT)

- Who gives some years but unfortunately not yet this year? (SYBUNT)

STORY #9 *Donor Data Management*

Data mining.

We sat down with a contribution list of people who had made gifts of $5000 or more over the last five years to the Community Arts Fund in a small town in Ohio.

*I asked who **the** most passionate supporter was on the list.*

After much discussion everyone agreed it was someone who had given nearly three years ago but not yet this year. The contributor, George, was the executive director's best friend.

George had made his gift because his good friend, James, had invited him to do so. George had a few interactions with staff and board at the Community Arts Fund, but no one had really spent much time with him. He'd retired with a good "package" from the company he worked at for more than 25 years.

A meeting was set with George. Delightful conversations were had. Advice was sought about how to finish off an endowment campaign that was critical to the Arts Fund.

Not only did George eventually make a $25,000 gift to the campaign, he agreed to spearhead the efforts to wrap up the campaign. Last count more than $100,000 had been generated by George's efforts. And six months ago, he wasn't even on the radar.

All this from simply taking the time to review contribution data. The Community Arts Fund actually has a donor database that had been well tended with details about the relationship between George and James.

Pausing to regularly review donor data is key to building a successful fundraising campaign.

That's it! Nine steps to a successful fundraising campaign.

My suggestions:

- *Choose one area to tackle at a time.*
- *Talk about the people whose lives are different because of your work.*
- *Talk about the MONEY. Please.*

Your supporters and those waiting to support you will thank you! I promise.

IN REVIEW
NINE STEPS FOR SUCCESSFUL FUNDRAISING CAMPAIGN

STEP **#1** *Leadership*
Successful individual donor campaigns are led by key volunteer and/or staff leadership.

STEP **#2** *Staff*
Successful individual donor campaigns are supported and managed by at least one staff member.

STEP **#3** *Board Members*
Successful individual donor campaigns have all board members participating in fundraising in some capacity.

STEP **#4** *Goals, Timelines, and Urgency*
Successful individual donor campaigns have a well-defined goal, with a specific timeline, creating a sense of urgency.

STEP **#5** *Telling Your Story*
Successful individual donor campaigns create an emotional connection — making it personal for people to participate.

STEP **#6** *Keeping Your Donors Engaged*
Successful individual donor campaigns keep donors and interested parties informed and engaged.

STEP **#7** *Money Conversation*
Successful individual donor campaigns keep your money story visible to encourage widespread participation.

STEP **#8** *Be Specific*
Successful individual donor campaigns invite participants to do very specific things with a deadline for doing them.

STEP **#9** *Donor Data Management*
Successful individual donor campaigns use a donor data management system to track donor contacts and gifts.

RECOMMENDED RESOURCES

Money

The Soul of Money, Lynne Twist, W.W. Norton & Company Inc., originally published 2003. Updated 2017.

Fundraising & Communication

Complete Storytelling System, Lori L Jacobwith, 2014. Updated 2018.

The Essential Guide to Fundraising for Small Nonprofits, 2013.

Asking: A 59 Minute Guide to Everything Board Members, Volunteers & Staff Must Know to Secure the Gift, Jerold Panas, Emerson & Church, Publications, 2009.

Donor-Centered Fundraising: How to Hold On to Your Donors and Raise Much More Money, Penelope Burk, originally published 2003. Updated version 2018.

Yours For the Asking: An Indispensable Guide to Fundraising & Management, Reynold Levy, President, Lincoln Center for the Performing Arts, Wiley & Sons, 2008.

Forces for Good: The Six Practices of High-Impact Social profits, Leslie R. Crutchfield & Heather McLeod Grant, 2009.

Blogs and Free Resources

Fire Starters — IgnitedFundraising.com/blog

Ignited Fundraising Free ebooks:
* *Mission Possible — Your Workbook for a Successful Board*
* *Boring2Brilliant: Finding and Sharing Stories That Cause People to Take Action*

More free resources:
http://www.ignitedfundraising.com/training/free-resources/

ABOUT LORI

The first thing people notice when they meet Lori is her passion for the positive.

She helps find the "it's possible" angle to most any fundraising challenge.

Lori's gifts and talents help executive directors, development directors, and even fundraising committee chairs' communicate powerfully to exponentially increase their fundraising.

Named one of America's Top 25 Fundraising Experts, Lori L. Jacobwith is an internationally-recognized master storyteller and fundraising culture change expert.

Lori has more than 30 years' experience helping nonprofit organizations raise $300 million dollars from individual donors. And counting.

Not your average speaker or trainer, Lori's poise, humor, enthusiasm, and best practices inspire and electrify. She teaches how to connect with and engage others by doing the same herself.

By sharing easy-to-implement strategies and tools that will inspire even the most-weary or overworked nonprofit staff or board member, Lori make training sessions, keynotes, or board retreats effective and memorable.

A longtime member of the Association of Fundraising Professionals, Lori holds a BA from the University of Minnesota and additional training from Indiana University's Fund Raising School. It's true, Lori has a passion for fundraising — She also has a passion for attending her native Minnesota State Fair — for more than 50 consecutive years.